DESTINY
REVEALED

THE JOURNEY TO UNCOVER YOUR

PURPOSE,

HEALING,

AND VALUE

THROUGH JESUS

DR. MIKE COWEN

Warrior Notes Publishing
PO Box 1288
Destrehan, LA 70047

Cover design: Virtually Possible Designs

For more information about our school, go to www.warriornotesschool.com.

Reach us on the internet: www.Kevinzadai.com

ISBN 13: 978-1-6631-0096-2

ISBN eBook: 978-1-6631-0097-9

ISBN Audio: 978-1-6631-0098-6

CONTENTS

Foreword by Dr. Kevin L. Zadai 5

Introduction   Where It Begins 7

Chapter 1   Perceived Value 13

Chapter 2   False Labels 23

Chapter 3   Imposter? 29

Chapter 4   Leaving the Garage Sale 35

Chapter 5   Losing Control 41

Chapter 6   Trust, Hope, and Healing 53

Chapter 7   Your Seat at the Table 69

Chapter 8   Lost and Now Found 79

Chapter 9   Impartation Prayer 87

Chapter 10   Transformation Scriptures and
Declarations 91

About the Author 107

FOREWORD

I'm so thankful for everything God has done and continues to do through Pastor Mike Cowen's life. He's been an amazing friend and has worked really hard to make the vision God gave me for Warrior Notes come to pass. But more than that, he has a huge heart and wants to help people reach their God-given destinies.

Mike lives out what he teaches us in *Destiny Revealed* every day. God has shown him how incredibly valuable each and every believer is because of what Jesus did for us. If you're ready to breathe new life into the purpose God has for you, open your heart, and receive the vital message in this book. I truly believe it has the power to change your life. Let this book be a heavenly impartation and the unlocking of God's calling within you.

Kevin Zadai PhD

WHERE IT BEGINS

Thank you for taking this journey with me to be healed and transformed as you read this book. I cannot imagine all that you have been through and how hard you have fought to become the person your Father God has created you to be. I know, as you have pursued a relationship with Jesus, that you have encountered many different people, battles, and hardships. This is to be expected since we live in a fallen world with broken people. Thankfully, the wonderful news of hope is found in the gospel and all that Jesus has done for us through the shedding of His blood.

In this book we are going to walk through different areas of transformation by discovering the biblical value and identity that Jesus reveals in us. I want you to let the Holy Spirit delve deep into your heart and soul as you read the stories, scriptures, and revelation I share with you. I know that opening your heart in this way can be scary, as the world seems to just always steal, kill, and destroy. Jesus, though, wants to gain access to the bruised and bleeding places in your heart and soul to bring life.

So, how do we resolve these matters and move on? Let me share a story with you. My wife and I recently bought a little house, and I love it. However, the property was neglected for a while, and there was this massive pile of trees, bushes, and plywood. This pile stretched the length of three cars and was probably four to five feet tall. It was massive.

I decided to burn it. As I strategized how to do so safely, I waited for the perfect time: a week of rain followed by no wind. That week finally came. Afterwards was a sunny day, and the ground was still wet from the previous days of rain. I knew I could now control the fire so it would not turn into a massive fireball. So, I lit that pile on fire—and it burned and burned and burned. I literally had to manage this fire for days upon days. There's something about a fire, once you get it hot, that you're not going to put it out.

Because of the earlier days of rain and thus wet wood, the fire turned into this slow burn that was beneficial to me. I felt safer about the fire, but it took days to burn. The fire started on one side of the huge pile, then it moved to the other. The whole time I'm going outside and raking it. I'm doing my part to keep it nice and tight and to consolidate it. Finally, I got it down to one small pile.

Next to the huge mound that I had been burning were these three posts and some old firewood. The wood was all cut up, but there were all these vines in the stack. I thought to myself, *Now that I have accomplished my mission of the big pile, I'm going to work on this one.* Christine and I wanted to plant fruit trees and develop a garden on this part of the property, so the mess needed to go. If you don't clean out all the old rot and debris, how can you have room to create new life and growth?

Unfortunately, I made the mistake of thinking this was going to be easy. So, naive and energetic, I began to pull those posts out and get the old firewood removed. It was a train wreck! I struggled so much to pull anything out with those tightly wound vines... Why couldn't this just be easy?

I was trying to pull these chunks of wood out, but every time I tried to pull one, the vines deeply connected to the wood resisted. It was taking me all this work and effort when it looked like it would be easy. I went to the next level and got a machete. As I was hacking and whacking up these vines, in my head I was envisioning myself in the jungle, and it was me ver-sus this monstrosity. Finally, to my relief, I began to get some of the wood out, and I saw some pieces were rotten and some were good.

My intention was just to clean the land. I wanted to be like a pioneer and establish my homestead on my property, but I did not anticipate the battle and work it would take to accomplish this goal—just like the healing and deliverance of the heart.

I got all the firewood out, but half of the wood was rotted, so I separated them. Next, I decided to get the posts out. Now, they were just four-by-four posts. They were not cemented in, so I was thinking, *I've got this. No problem.* Little did I know that those posts were mocking me, literally mocking me. I pushed, pulled, rocked, and kicked them with no mercy. They just sat still, laughing at me. I decided, *Fine. I'll get leverage. Leverage is my friend.* So, I went and got this big crowbar. I drilled a hole into a post, got the crowbar into it, then got a carjack. Despite this masterpiece of physics that I made, the post did not move at all. Then it was time to go old school. I got my shovel out. And I dug, and I dug, and I dug, and I finally got the first post out. However, it was also wrapped in vines. Ugh!

There I was, with nasty wet and rotted wood, clingy vines, and immovable posts. When I got the first post out, I felt like a man for a moment. Then I went to the second post, and that one actually came out easily. Win! The third post, however, was the same scenario as the first post. You get the picture now: more digging...

Phew! Victory at last! I stood there looking at the battle-field in my yard. I had my post; I had rotten wood; I had vines; I had tree branches. Everything was lying around everywhere. I looked at it all, then said to myself, *"How am I going to sort all this out? What a mess!"* Then these words flew out of my mouth: "Forget it. I'm just going to let the fire take care of it." Wow! Immediately I was taken aback at the words that had come out of my mouth. I knew it was the Holy Spirit speaking to me. I looked at it all—all the work and all the mess that was made—and said it again. "I am going to let the fire take care of it all."

This pile of brush, overgrowth, and old wood represents what happens inside of us as believers. Piles grow, trees grow, vines grow, things grow. They grow because of a concept I want to introduce to you: neglect. I don't think we talk enough about neglect. We don't want to talk about it because we are all working so hard already. We're trying to maintain. We're trying to keep the car between the lanes, but meanwhile we're putting off the oil change. We're putting off the tire change that we need. We're putting off that "check engine" light. And while we are neglecting ourselves, our healing, our relationship with Jesus, and everything else continue to escalate and grow into something that can take us out. The neglect of our hearts and the traumas that get embedded in our souls are just like these piles in my story. How many years did the former owners just leave it? I am wondering, whatever you are facing, is now the time to let the fire of His love take care of it? Just turn the page, and we will walk into revelation and healing together.

CHAPTER I

PERCEIVED VALUE

Behold what manner of love the Father has bestowed on us, that we should be called children of God! Therefore the world does not know us, because it did not know Him. Beloved, now we are children of God; and it has not yet been revealed what we shall be, but we know that when He is revealed, we shall be like Him, for we shall see Him as He is.

—1 John 3:1–2

Several years ago, I heard a story about a family who loved going to yard sales. This family went to a particular yard sale and noticed a very plain serving bowl. The bowl was white with a few small markings around the edges, yet it was interesting. They ended up paying thirty-five dollars for this simple bowl. The bowl sat on a shelf for many years, overlooked and collecting dust just like any other yard sale item would. One day, a friend of the family was at their house, and he looked at the bowl and noticed something peculiar about it.

He mentioned to the family that something looked interesting about it and that they should look further into its value and origin. However, the family dismissed the promptings of their friend because they felt that it was "just a bowl" and probably was not even worth what they had paid for it.

Several years went by, and finally one of the family members decided to have the bowl appraised. To the person's shock and amazement, that plain yard sale find was a 1,000-year-old Ming Dynasty pottery bowl. The auctioneer deemed that it was worth at least $200,000 to $300,000! Naturally, all the family members were shocked. How could a simple yard sale bowl that spent years sitting on a shelf be worth hundreds of thousands of dollars?

The family eventually listed the bowl at an auction with great anticipation. There was quite a stir when multiple people began bidding on it. As the enthusiasm for the auction increased, so did the bids, higher and higher! There was so much excitement over this simple yard sale item. When the gavel finally fell, that plain, insignificant, unappreciated bowl sold for over $700,000!

So many of us are like that magnificent bowl today.

That plain bowl just sat on the shelf for many years—an absolute treasure—because it had been severely misvalued. It sat there for years because the family thought its value was based on where they bought it and how much they had paid for it. I am sure they also thought that its price tag was reasonable based on all the other low-value items surrounding it. The family thought that its perceived value was fact. If the bowl was carelessly put out at a yard sale and priced accordingly, then it must be worth only the price they paid and nothing more. However, as we found out, the perceived value was very wrong. That bowl had far greater value than anyone had ever anticipated!

Many people judge their own value based on their surroundings—just like this bowl at a yard sale. Some people feel very little personal value and self-worth because their surroundings have led them to believe their perceived value is their actual value. For instance, whatever store you shop at represents a certain level of quality. If you are at a budget store, then you expect budget items. If you are at a high-end store, then you expect quality items.

What kind of surroundings were you raised in? Maybe you grew up in a poor environment. Perhaps you grew up in a wealthy gated community. No matter what area of the spectrum you have found yourself to be in—whether wealthy, middle class, impoverished or any other grouping—you tend to perceive your value based on the type of environment you were raised in. People base their value on where they have come from, how they were raised, what they have been through, and where they have ended up in life. They often mislabel and misvalue themselves and others. Unfortunately, most don't realize that the value others placed on them, or they placed on themselves is not correct—it's not how God sees them. If you have gone through life believing that your value is based on the amount of money you have, your family history, your physical attributes, the number of friends you have, or what kind of job you ended up with, then you have misvalued yourself. Unfortunately, all of us have misjudged and misvalued ourselves to the point that we discredit the wonderful work Jesus did for us on the cross. We discredit the cross by the things we say and the way we treat ourselves and others.

Do you feel that people have misvalued or mislabeled you? People have certainly done that to me. It's as if someone tried to put a price tag on me, and suddenly I was faced with a decision. Would I accept it or reject it? I pray that, as you read this book, the "price tags" and false labels that have been placed on you begin to be removed, and, in their place, you discover your true value and identity through Jesus. This revelation will transform your entire life, as it has mine.

One day my wife and I went on a date to eat at a nice restaurant. Even though the restaurant was busy and full of people, we were enjoying ourselves. Our waitress was doing a great job taking care of our orders, and as I was noticing how hard she was working, I felt the Holy Spirit tugging at my heart to pay attention to what was happening at the table next to us. The couple that was seated near us began to verbally lash out at our waitress. In a very smug tone, they addressed the waitress, saying, "Where is our food? It's been ten minutes!" I thought to myself, *I just heard you order two minutes ago!* They were treating this waitress as if she was their servant and should obey their every command.

Just then, another table full of people started demanding things from the waitress. Those people were getting up from the table multiple times and asking the waitress for things that were really no big deal and completely over the top. It was a terrible atmosphere, and I was getting increasingly upset in my spirit! As I was observing all the chaos happening around us, I began to wonder what was *really* going on.

Unfortunately, it did not stop there. A few moments later, the same waitress was cleaning another table with no one around her. A lady got up from her seat near us and walked all the way over to the waitress and said, "Can you stop cleaning that table? I don't like the smell, and it's disturbing my meal." The waitress was taken aback and speechless, as the table she was cleaning was across the room from where this lady was seated, but then she said, "Okay, I will clean it later." The lady then went back to her seat and sat down with a smirk on her face as if to say *I sure told her!* I just looked at that lady and thought to myself, *Who are you? Who do you think you are that you have the right to treat someone that way?* I couldn't believe how so many different people were treating this innocent waitress like trash.

My spirit rose within me as I was taking it all in. Then, suddenly, I knew what was happening and why it was happening. I also knew I had to do something about it. I waited for the waitress to come back to our table, and I did not give my wife fair warning as to what I was going to say next. When the waitress came over to us, I looked at her and said, "Ma'am, I have been watching how these people have been treating you, and I am sorry." She replied, "Well, who complained?" She had immediately thrown up her defenses because she thought I was going to do the same thing to her that everyone else had been doing. I said, "No one. I just watched how all those people were treating you. That was wrong, and I'm sorry."

I just knew I had to say something to her. I felt Father God's compassion for her. (Compassion is the key to unlocking the prophetic. Compassion will unlock your spirit so you can reach out to the people around you. Remember how compassion unlocked miracles through Jesus? If you desire to be used in the prophetic but don't have compassion, you could move into dangerous territory.) In that moment, I released that simple word of apology over her, and it shook her. It shook all of us because we all felt a release of God's love and compassion for her.

After I apologized to her, she stared at me speechless. I could tell that she was trying to understand what was happening at that moment. Then she was able to get these words out: "This has been happening to me my whole life." I felt God's love for her flow through me, and I saw the reality of the cycle that she was experiencing every day. I said to her, "You are worth more than all of this, and God has a plan for your life." Tears began to well up in her eyes, and she quickly walked away. I could see so many emotions in her rising to the surface.

My wife looked at me and asked, "What just happened?" I answered, "This was a release of the love of God, and His love directly confronted the cycles of this waitress's mistreatment. This entire situation was an attack on her value and worth." We finished our meal, leaving the waitress a large tip and writing on the receipt a simple little note that Jesus loved her and had a wonderful plan for her life.

That young waitress had been harassed by the enemy her entire life. The enemy had used people to try to erode her value to the point that being abused by people was normal to her. By the time I had the privilege of meeting her, it was obvious that she had allowed her value to be completely degraded. Just like that bowl in our story, this precious waitress had "been at the garage sale" for so long that she had begun to think and feel that she was only worth a few dollars. When you think you are only worth a few dollars, you allow people to treat you like you are only worth those few dollars.

When people get to the point in their life when they look in the mirror and don't like what they see on the outside or how they feel on the inside, they stop taking care of themselves and no longer love themselves. The world has eroded their hearts to the point that they no longer see themselves as God sees them. The enemy wants you to identify with your broken surroundings and your mislabels. Like that garage sale bowl, the enemy wants you to put a false price tag on yourself so that you never really know your great value and worth. My friend, Jesus gave His life for you. You are His priceless treasure that He purchased with His blood. It is time to begin to identify and remove those false price tags that this broken world has tried to get you to accept.

> *For we are His workmanship, created in Christ Jesus for good works, which God prepared before-hand that we should walk in them.*
> —**Ephesians 2:10**

Just as the Lord sent me and my wife to that precious wait-ress to minister to her, God has commissioned me to tell you that you are God's workmanship and His beloved child! The world is continually trying to bring you down to its level. It's this low level that causes God's workmanship—me and you—to live mislabeled and undervalued if we allow those lies in our lives. Jesus gave His blood to redeem us. All of us were at one time lost, but now we have been found. In finding us, Father God has restored our hearts, our value, and our purpose in Him.

PRAY WITH ME:

Dear Jesus, thank You for the blood. I thank You for giving Your life for me. Help me to see the value You have placed inside me. I am tired of the false price tags and labels that people have put on me. Forgive me for accepting those as my own. Bring revelation to my heart that my value and worth are defined only by what You think and feel about me and by those things that are written in Your Word. Thank You for revealing Your love for me now. In Jesus's name, Amen!

Now let's look at your life. Take a moment and share your thoughts on what the Holy Spirit is revealing to you through these stories by answering the following questions.

Have you seen any cycles in the way you are treated?

_____

_____

_____

_____

**What incorrect values and labels
have been placed on you?**

_____

_____

_____

_____

**How has the enemy used repeat scenarios
to erode your identity and value?**

_____

_____

_____

_____

CHAPTER 2

FALSE LABELS

I grew up going to church. Around the age of seventeen, God got a hold of me. How many of us have seen that when God gets a hold of someone, a lot of devils freak out? They start getting loud because they don't want to lose that person. When I got saved, my friends and I started evangelizing our whole high school. We were holding prayer meetings and doing outreach. We were not doing anything half-baked because we were sold out for Jesus. It was wonderful. However, I found this theme of mislabeling happening in my life even during that time.

I had so much joy, and that seemed to be a beacon to the enemy. I had struggled with feeling loved. I had struggled with value. I had struggled with all these issues, but when I found Jesus, all my life questions were answered. Finding Jesus resolved all of those things for me. So, therefore, I was happy. I was excited. I actually believed what the Bible said about my new life and my relationship with Jesus. I believed people could be healed. I believed that God had a plan for my life. I believed I could do what He was putting in my heart. However, what I didn't know was that this newfound joy and freedom were going to stir things up in a lot of people. I didn't know that my freedom would trigger their identity problems.

Like a record player, people would continually tell me about how much pride I had inside of me. "Mike, that's pride. This is pride. That is pride." I heard it so much that I started thinking, *If everybody's saying I have pride, then I must have a real problem.* The next thing I knew, I had decided that I was going to rid myself of this pride. I began to throw things away. I had trophies from competitive archery and shooting, and I got rid of them. I began to get rid of the clothes I liked to wear. I just cut out all these things I loved because I thought that I had pride in my life and that I needed to deal with that pride.

Looking back, I realize that I had freedom and the joy of the Lord in my life, and because people didn't know how to handle that, they attacked it. They didn't know what to do with me, so they labeled me as prideful.

I believe you know what I am talking about, that you can relate my experiences to your own. You have been falsely labeled like I have. You have been falsely labeled by people and things in this world just like Jesus was. Let me tell you, as a father and a pastor, if anybody is quick to label you without knowing you, be cautious about heeding what that person is telling you.

People act the way they do often because they've been through a lot, and what they have been through can affect how they view the people around them. They themselves have been misvalued and labeled, so they do the same thing to others without realizing it. Just as you don't want people to write you off, don't write off those who have treated you wrongly, even if what they have done was hurtful. What you can do is take them out for coffee and spend a little time with them. Love them and let them talk so you can get to know them. When you do that, you will find that they have been through something, and they need somebody who is willing to get past that and love them. If everybody had somebody who would reach into their heart and life, we would be able to see just how much quality is in every individual. Think about it. If this is what is happening to you, might you also be doing this to others unknowingly?

> *Therefore, whatever you want men to do to you, do also to them, for this is the Law and the Prophets.*
> **—Matthew 7:12**

I was labeled with pride and other things, and it took me decades to get rid of them all. How many of you can relate to that? It can take time to get those labels off of you, for what happens when you identify with them? You become them. You begin to talk like those labels, act like those labels, and think like those labels. Have you ever looked at a clearance item and seen how many times it has been marked down? It started with one price, yet, with label after label, the value went down, down, down.

Do you feel this way? You have had so many labels put on you, and each label just lowered your value until it could not get any lower. But the gospel of Jesus is the good news that those labels are wrong and that you are His priceless child. The deliverance that Jesus offers you today is your total freedom—you can let go of what has been said and done to you and receive the love and value that God has placed in you.

Again, the kingdom of heaven is like treasure hidden in a field, which a man found and hid; and for joy over it he goes and sells all that he has and buys that field.

—Matthew 13:44

We, as believers, know that Jesus is our treasure. He is our beautiful Savior, and He has given His life for us so we can be born again. Accepting Jesus is so simple that a child can receive Him. This is why many people struggle with the gospel. Their mind wants to make it more than just receiving forgiveness because they've been through so many rounds of labels. As a result, they identify with difficulties, complications, and struggles. When they identify with struggles, they subconsciously want things to be hard. Because they want things to be difficult, they try to make the gospel difficult. They make healing hard. They make praying in tongues hard. They make helping people hard because life has been hard. God made the gospel simple and light because His love for us is pure and uncomplicated. The transformation process Paul talks about in the book of Romans is meant to take the complicated out of us—to heal us and deliver us from the brokenness that has come because of the fall of Adam and Eve. We need to be renewed by His love!

We've preached a lot of candy and sugar messages in our churches. Those messages taste good at first but leave us hungry for truth. We need to know how to change. We need to know that we *can* change. We need to know that we are forgiven. We need to know that our past has been resolved and that there is a ministry waiting for all of us. We don't need to feel better for only a moment; rather, we need the labels and hurt permanently removed so we can receive love and give love. This is what Jesus has done for us—He has restored our value and destiny. We must remember that when we found Jesus, He found us as well. We are His treasure.

He left the glory of Heaven to find His lost treasure...you.

PRAY WITH ME:

Father God, I take off every false label and word that has been put on me. I no longer accept an identity of struggle, worthlessness, and hopelessness. I choose to receive Your love and value for me. You are my treasure, and I am Yours. Amen.

Take a moment to turn your attention inward. Write your answers to the following questions.

**What was the Holy Spirit revealing to
you while you read this chapter?**

_____

_____

_____

_____

How have you identified with false labels?

_____

_____

_____

_____

**What are two new ways you will begin to
see your identity as it is found in Jesus?**

_____

_____

_____

_____

CHAPTER 3

IMPOSTER?

I remember the day my oldest daughter went to college. We were so proud and excited for her. It was a beautiful day and such a wonderful campus. We were all gathered to hear the president of the university address the new students and welcome them. He was getting everyone to laugh and feel like family at their new home. Then he took a turn in his speech and began to address the feelings they were having and would be facing while on this new journey. He dug into their hearts to share with them about "imposter syndrome." I had not heard that term before, so I was all ears to hear where he was heading with this topic. He talked about the many different walks of life that were represented in this new class and the many first-generation college students who were in the group.

What he was trying to get them to understand was that they belonged there—that the feelings and thoughts that they were not good enough or did not belong were not true. Even if they came from poverty and no one in their family had ever taken the path of earning a college education before, that did not mean they were there by accident.

Have you ever felt this way as a Christian? I believe most have. When we go on the journey to discover our inheritance in Jesus, we fight the thoughts of *I don't deserve this* and *I don't belong here.* We fight these thoughts from this broken world that have gotten into us. Like a broken compass, they tell us the wrong direction every time.

Think about the bowl from the garage sale that we talked about in the first chapter. Imagine with me for a moment that the bowl could talk and tell its story. It would tell us how people put a low value and expectation on it, how it was surrounded by other common items and people assumed it was just like the others—nothing special and nothing beautiful. Now, imagine the bowl on the auction table at Sotheby's. Imagine its journey from the garage sale table to the auction table. Now, everyone wants it, and its price tag has lots of "zeros" added to it. I can only imagine, if that bowl could talk, it would say, "You're bidding on the wrong item," and, "I am not worth that much." That bowl would have been comfortable with garage sales and simply holding a salad, but not with being priceless!

Sometimes, as people, we have a hard time truly believing what Jesus has done for us. We seem to know it; we can teach it; but do we believe it in our hearts? Has our mind been renewed with this truth? In a broken world where things seem to be in total chaos, we are now living with the complete, whole, and perfect love of God. The contrast between the realities of Heaven and the work of the cross with the realities of this realm and broken world we are operating in is huge. They are polar opposites.

Let's go back to the term imposter syndrome. What is it, and how does it affect you? Let's say you inherit a million dollars. You look at your bank account, and you see the balance of $1,000,000. You can see the fact that your bank account really has that much money in it. Yet, on the inside, you still feel poor and are still looking at when the next paycheck will be deposited—all despite the fact of your actual bank account balance.

You go to the store and buy just enough food for a few days. You run through the drive-thru and order something from the budget menu. At the gas pump, you only put in five dollars' worth because your instinct is to do what you have always done to survive. Even though you have a million dollars in the bank, which is a fact, you feel like you must pinch every penny, or you won't make it. Accepting your new account balance and living differently would make you feel like an imposter.

Do you struggle with imposter syndrome? Think about it. You are forgiven. This is the truth of Heaven. Your spirit is perfect, clean, and now whole! But do you live and make all of your decisions out of this truth? Or do you second-guess yourself? A lot of believers struggle to move into this next step—to accept forgiveness and then live forgiven. Do you live forgiven? It's easy to say you do but pause with me and reflect for a moment. If nothing is holding you back and nothing is hindering you, what decisions would you make to change your future? Would you learn something new? Would you start a business or a ministry? How would you help and love people? What limitations would you throw off?

Do you struggle with wanting to step out to do all the things God has put in your heart? Do you think people will try and tell you who you are and what you can and can't do? Today, could you take a step of faith and accept that Jesus removed all the limits and is not holding you back? Let me share this truth with you: what holds you back is what you believe about yourself.

> *For with God nothing will be impossible.*
> —Luke 1:37

God is ready to help you remove your limits. He didn't put them there, and He wants you to take them off. You can play instruments. You can write. You can help people and bring change. You can do absolutely anything that God puts in your heart. If God has put some dream in your heart, He's going to give you everything you need to complete it. You were made to do remarkable things. You are not an imposter for stepping out into the greatness of God's love and calling in your life. Your value is not found in the things you have or the places you have been. Your declared value is based on who God has made you to be and the treasure that has been placed within you.

It's time to identify with the heavenly treasures and not the garage sale price tags of this world. You are not an imposter for believing what God has declared over you. You are priceless. This is why there has been a war for you. The enemy never wanted you to get here and see your true beauty. Well, guess what? The enemy has lost because you made it, and you are now looking at the value of Heaven inside of you! You are not a fake trying to pretend. You are truly a child of the King!

Heaven's kingdom realm can be illustrated like this: A person discovered that there was hidden treasure . . .

—Matthew 13:44 (TPT)

PRAY AND DECLARE WITH ME:

Jesus, from this moment forward, I will begin to see the value and treasure You have placed within me. I am not an imposter. I am truly Your child, called to make a difference. I choose to see Your love and the potential that is now my position as a believer. In Jesus's name, Amen.

Pause and consider these questions. Take the time to really think about your answers.

**What about God's love and forgiveness
do you struggle to accept?**

_____

_____

_____

_____

**What would you love to start or do
again if you had no limits?**

_____

_____

_____

_____

**What thoughts do you think about yourself
that you would like to change?**

_____

_____

_____

_____

CHAPTER 4

LEAVING THE GARAGE SALE

Knowing that you were not redeemed with corruptible things, like silver or gold, from your aimless conduct received by tradition from your fathers, but with the precious blood of Christ, as of a lamb without blemish and without spot.

—1 Peter 1:18-19

N ow, let's settle this together. You were misplaced by this world. You were sent to the garage sale and labeled incorrectly. You are a priceless piece of God's treasure, but you were misplaced and mismarked. So, our next step is to get you out of this place. We need to get this type of wrong thinking and false reality out of you. We need to get you to where you belong and help you see the appropriate value in your identity. For this to happen, you must believe what Jesus believes about you. Jesus left His Father and His home to find His missing treasures: us. When He came to our world, He gave everything to buy us back. He searched every garage sale, every bar, and every corner to find His lost treasures. He did not leave us in this broken and lost state; He shed His blood to redeem us. No man would give everything for an item that is common. No one would give up everything unless the value was truly there and just waiting to be found and restored.

Jesus gave His life for you. He didn't give His life for garbage. He gave His life for something way more precious than silver and gold. He gave His life because you are a son, because you are a daughter, and it's time for you to take your rightful place. It's now time for you to start thinking like He does. Changing your thinking will change how you make your daily decisions—no more living in the mental pigpen. Heaven's treasures should not be lying in the mud of this world. You have been called to the King's palace. You have been called up to the King's table. Stop thinking and feeling like you only deserve to be on the clearance rack and believing that is who you are. Choose life today, and don't go back!

> *But God, who is rich in mercy, because of His great love with which He loved us, even when we were dead in trespasses, made us alive together with Christ (by grace you have been saved).*
>
> **—Ephesians 2:4-5**

Treasure goes with treasure. If this is how He sees you, and if this is the price He paid for you, then it is a horrible disgrace to see yourself at the garage sale table. It's time for you to now identify with life! His life is a gift to you. You no longer have to live in "survival mode" because you are now alive in Christ. You are moving up to sit at the table of the Lord and to dine with Him. You are moving towards your reserved seat with Him. To take that first step towards your seat, however, you must be convinced in your heart and mind that you belong there.

Let's address the thoughts of, *How do I do this?* and, *I still don't have enough to pay my bills!* I know it can be easy to say, "Be His treasure," but hard to believe in your heart when you are thinking, *How do I act like His treasure when I am eating ramen noodles?* Knowing you are a treasure is not just an outward position you take and begin to demand your rights. It starts in your spirit. Your spirit needs to be released to let the flow of His Spirit come in and through you. When you do this, when you let go, you begin the transformation process. Your soul (which is your mind, will, and emotions) has been very comfortable with the fall. It has been fine with the way it identifies with sin, traumas, and brokenness. It has been "at home" with this lifestyle. So, to receive the treasures of Heaven, you must begin by opening up the treasure chest, which is the Word of God. The Bible is the mirror you need to look into so you can see yourself as you really are: loved, wanted, and needed in this generation.

As you allow the Word to reflect God's heart and plans for you, your spirit begins to connect and release them through your soul. At first, your soul will throw out all kinds of reasons for why these truths are wrong. When you begin to see that you are loved by God, your soul wants to remind you of all the times you were not loved in this life... and it can be a war. For many of us, our soul has been hurt and traumatized in so many ways that we find layers upon layers that the Holy Spirit wants and needs to restore within us. We will work through this process in this book. The Holy Spirit is ready to teach, comfort, and bring you through.

> *For we are His workmanship, created in Christ Jesus for good works, which God prepared beforehand that we should walk in them.*
>
> **—Ephesians 2:10**

PRAY WITH ME:

Jesus, ignite my heart with the fire of Your love. I choose to leave behind all the old ways that I would see myself. I no longer identify with the old me. Let my sprit be one with You and begin the transformation in me. My soul has been through so much, God. Yet, I know that You have put a treasure inside me. Today, let the real me begin to come forth in You. Amen.

Let your heart respond to these questions. Be as honest as you can so the healing can begin.

How do I think Jesus sees me and feels about me?

_____

_____

_____

_____

What beautiful things has Jesus placed in me?

_____

_____

_____

_____

What excites me the most about my future with Jesus?

_____

_____

_____

_____

CHAPTER 5

LOSING CONTROL

Surely goodness and mercy shall follow me all the days of my life; and I will dwell in the house of the LORD forever.

—Psalm 23:6

Everyone reading this book has probably, at one time or another, prayed and asked God to do a great work in him or her. Maybe you are praying for it, wanting it, and doing everything you can to obtain it. Let me assure you that you are doing the right things to walk in favor. However, what I see holding many believers back are things they have not let go of yet. Let me be your heart doctor as you read and help you navigate what the Holy Spirit is saying to you. If you will allow it, then I know that by the end of this process, a real healing will take place. I know that a real deliverance will take place. You are at the door of your transformation as you read and take this principle to heart. It is going to be the next step that many of you have been praying for and asking God for.

What I'm talking about is *letting go*. I am not talking about sin issues. I am talking about hooks that are in your heart—places, times, and people that you have been tethered to. When trauma, loss, and pain happen, you get tethered to those times and places. You get tied to those moments you have gone through. You may find yourself frustrated or exhausted because you're not moving forward each day. You can't move forward until you become unhooked from the moments that have altered and hurt you. I ask you, as you read this and the following chapters, to open your heart, step back, and let the Holy Spirit minister to you. I invite you to take notes or highlight as you read. As we move forward together, there will be some powerful moments of revelation. I know the Holy Spirit will minister to you.

First, let's look at the beginning of Psalm 23. We are all very comfortable with Psalm 23. Most people understand or have a general knowledge of this passage of Scripture. The problem is the gap we see between where our life is and where Psalm 23 declares it should be. This gap seems to appear in most of our hearts, our emotions, and our bodies. Nevertheless, our Father has provided many benefits for us in Psalm 23.

> *The LORD is my shepherd; I shall not want. He makes me to lie down in green pastures; He leads me beside the still waters.*
>
> **—Psalm 23:1-2**

We should be enjoying the life of green pastures. We should be receiving refreshing, healing springs of life. He leads us into new seasons of life and wholeness! Still waters are safe. When our Shepherd brings us to a place of healing and rejuvenation, we can be assured that He is on guard against the wolves and will alert us if our attention is needed.

> *He restores my soul; He leads me in the paths of righteousness for His name's sake.*
>
> **—Psalm 23:3**

This verse declares that you can have restoration on a constant, continual basis. Your path should be taking you to good places. This verse is not saying that you *went* to good places. It's saying you *are going* to good places. Therefore, if all those bad things are moments in your past, then you need to choose to let them go. His leading is to take you away from your past and into abundant life and destiny.

> *Yea, though I walk through the valley of the shadow of death, I will fear no evil; for You are with me; Your rod and Your staff, they comfort me.*
>
> **—Psalm 23:4**

Are you fighting the fear of evil? His rod and His staff are here to comfort you. In case you think that the rod and staff are here to beat you, let me assure you that they are not. His rod and His staff are to lead you. They are to beat off the wolves that have come to steal, to kill, and to destroy. Your Father has these safeguards in place because you are His precious child, and He is ready to defend and cover you.

You prepare a table before me in the presence of my enemies; You anoint my head with oil; my cup runs over.

—**Psalm 23:5**

We should be dining in the glory of God even if we are still living in the world! We should be partaking and engaging in Heaven's dinner table of life. We can be partakers of the divine nature. Our cup can now be found running over. Many have accepted a "normal" that is not Heaven's normal. Jesus didn't die for us to have the world's version of "normal"; He died for us to enjoy Heaven's normal. Our ability as believers is to continually go after and pursue the greater things. Through Jesus, we can now obtain the things that God has for us and not accept the brokenness and failings of this life, even if those things were our fault!

Surely goodness and mercy shall follow me all the days of my life.

—**Psalm 23:6a**

Goodness and mercy should be following you. Every time you look behind you, you should say, "Hello, goodness!" Not, "Oh my, my past!" As a child of the King, you can look behind you and say, "I'm going to be just fine because I have goodness and mercy with me." When somebody says something negative about you, or you get a bad report, or you get a bill, then you should be taking those things to prayer and saying, "Goodness and mercy, I have something for you to take care of!" This is walking in abundance. Every one of us should and can have this abundance in our life.

Why don't we have it? How can we get it? The answer is in letting go. You see, it's not that Psalm 23 is not in full effect; it is! It is God's Word. It is eternal. Everything else may fade away, but God's Word will stand forever. (See Matthew 24:35, for example.) So, if the problem is not God's Word, or the work of the cross, or the blood of Jesus, then what is it that keeps us from having these things in our daily life? What keeps us from pursuing the greater things? It's the wrong beliefs and limitations embedded in our souls. It's the things we need to let go of. So, let's challenge the barriers we have wrongly accepted.

The first issue we need to address is regarding control. Many of us have different levels of control problems in our lives. We have these control problems because of what we've been through. We also can think we can regain control by being controlling. Did you just say, "Ouch!"? You may wonder why I am bringing up this issue. It is because, in God, there is no fruit of control. It's not one of the fruits of the Spirit. Control and manipulation are not listed in Galatians. Yet, control is what most struggle with, even if it's in secret and covered with a smile and survival. When we've been through hard things, when this life has beaten us up, our instant human reaction is to take it and grab control of it. However, what often happens is that we try to gain control so much that we don't let our Father have control. When we grab the helm like that, we tend to steer our ships into storms and reefs and get off His map.

Dr. Kevin Zadai told me one time that "pride is self-reliance." The enemy has been working hard to get us into self-reliance.

When we operate in self-reliance, we are causing the Holy Spirit to be put on standby, waiting for you to let Him come back in and lead. This is our pain turned into pride. Pride says, "I'm going to do it my way." It does not matter what the motive is or if someone has hurt you. That is why pride is demonic and so blinding. It wounds you and then hands you the blade. Now, if I were to ask you, "Do you have pride?" most people would say, "No, I definitely do not." I mean, that's my first reaction. "Pride? No way." It is interesting how self-reliance enters through the things we've been through. We try to take control of our lives because this world has tried to take control of us and take control from us. However, our lives are not our own anymore; we don't take back control by being controlling. We take back control by letting go...

I used to think letting go meant I would just give everything to God and wait for Him to move, but that's not what "control by letting go" is. Letting go of control looks like this: You're on a ship, you're standing at the helm, and you're a yielded vessel. God says, "Take it a little left. Take it a little right. Go faster. Go slower. Drop your anchor. Pick up your anchor. Dock the boat. Undock the boat." And you obey. Now you are in a place of obedience because love is obedience. You love Him, and He loves you. You know that obeying Him will yield the best fruit in your life. Obedience will take you to Psalm 23.

Let's grow into a place where we are more yielded to the Holy Spirit and no longer yielded to this world, to our emotions, or to our mind. This world is not our home, so we should not operate as the world operates. We must operate in the realities of Heaven. When we surrender, we do not control. Rather, we gain order. God wants us to have His order. This is why I find most people struggle with control. We fight with everyone around us because we think control means we won't be hurt or abused again. I think we can honestly all say that we feel this world is fighting us to take control. But the kingdom of Heaven does not operate in the world's push and pull. The kingdom's flow of order and harmony is a well of life from the Spirit of God. When we have order in our life, then there's peace and joy! I personally believe this issue with control is why believers struggle with the flow of the fruits of the Spirit in their life. They can get in a system of control instead of a system of obedience and order. Does this describe you? The Holy Spirit wants to move into your life, and He wants to help you bring order. This is what your soul thirsts for.

When Adam and Eve were in the Garden of Eden, everything was perfectly in order. Their bodies worked correctly. Their minds worked perfectly. Their emotions worked in harmony. The world worked as designed. Everything was in Heaven's order. Unfortunately, the fall caused sin and brokenness. Brokenness brought control and manipulation. It all went downhill from there. When Jesus rose from the dead, He bought back our dominion. The order has been restored, yet it is not from the outside in. Rather, it flows from within you out to this world. You manifest the gifts and fruits of the Spirit because the dominion and order has been restored in and though you.

Prophetically speaking, what you're longing for is order inside yourself. In your life, your finances, your family, and your body. If you're in the medical field, then you understand these things. If your body is out of balance, you can't just take control and tell it what to do. Instead, you gently bring it back into harmony. You bring it back into order. If you're lacking vitamins or nutrients, then you need to add them back into your diet. That's why you never gain order back in your body and your emotions by beating them into submission.

If you deal with mental torment, then you may have demons harassing you. Or you might have hormones and imbalances that need to be addressed. Analyze every area with the Holy Spirit for it is a fallen, broken world. I believe demonic spirits will use your lack of knowledge against you, causing the cycle of sickness and harassment that torments you. That's why you need to be a student of the Word and research it. Go on a journey to know and understand the heart, character, and nature of God. When you know Him and His love for you, you take dominion back in your life and drive out the demonic. When you free yourself from past traumas and mindsets, it causes you to restore the order in your heart and free yourself from torment.

Keeping that tight grip on control hinders us from receiving what the Holy Spirit has for us. I know this is true because I've had to look in the mirror and say, "Mike, loosen up the grip. Loosen up the control and let God teach you and heal you." When I found that I couldn't let go of something, I learned that it was because I got hurt. It was because I got wounded. I went through something hard, and my soul wanted to gain order back, but the fallen nature wanted me to try and take it back by taking control. It didn't work. We need to pursue

God's order in our lives, not control. We need to pursue kingdom dominion, not selfish agendas to try to survive.

We now have a choice. We can keep operating the way we have been and produce the same fruit, or we can stop trying to beat control with control. When we stop trying to beat control with control, we let love and order preserve our hearts so that we can live in the fullness of the resurrection.

> *Not that I have already attained, or am already perfected; but I press on, that I may lay hold of that for which Christ Jesus has also laid hold of me. Brethren, I do not count myself to have apprehended; but one thing I do, forgetting those things which are behind and reaching forward to those things which are ahead, I press toward the goal for the prize of the upward call of God in Christ Jesus.*
> —Philippians 3:12–14

Today we are going to let go and let God's healing love flow into us, healing our hearts and souls, so that we can free ourselves from trying to control the pain.

Good-bye pain; good-bye control.
Hello, peace! Hello, joy! Hello, hope!

Declare this with me: "I am now allowing God's freedom to flow into every trauma. I receive Heaven's order in every area of my life. I will never be the same, in Jesus's name!"

PRAY THIS IMPARTATION
PRAYER WITH ME:

Father, thank You that You have order for me—a
safe place of being led and loved by You so I
don't have to be afraid. As I step back, I ask You
for revelation on every area that pain has driven
me to control. I want to gain healing and Your
order in my life. Heal me. Cover me. Bring me
back to Psalm 23 as You lead me and guide me,
with mercy and truth covering behind my steps.
I take back Your order in my life today, in Jesus's
name.

Take a moment to answer the following questions with honesty and transparency.

What areas in your life have you seen that you fight control?

_____

_____

_____

_____

How have pain and control kept you from moving forward in your life?

_____

_____

_____

_____

How will you now take Heaven's order back in your life?

_____

_____

_____

_____

CHAPTER 6

TRUST, HOPE, AND HEALING

H ave you ever said, "What is God doing in my life?" I think Abraham could qualify as one who had questions in his life as God was directing him. As we study more about letting go and trusting the leading of the Holy Spirit, it is so comforting to look at fathers of our faith who teach us about trust. In Genesis 22, we learn about Abraham and Isaac and their incredible journey of faith. This moment in their lives forever sealed their path with God, and it teaches us so much about God's nature. It also is an incredible type and shadow of the Messiah, Jesus. Studying this story will help us to go deeper into understanding our valuable destiny. The Word of God is such a beautiful mirror for our hearts and lives. This particular moment, I believe, is a prophetic mirror for us today. Let's begin with these two sections of Scripture:

> *Now it came to pass after these things that God tested Abraham, and said to him, "Abraham" And he said, "Here I am." Then He said, "Take now*

your son, your only son Isaac, whom you love, and go to the land of Moriah, and offer him there as a burnt offering on one of the mountains of which I shall tell you." So Abraham rose early in the morning and saddled his donkey, and took two of his young men with him, and Isaac his son; and he split the wood for the burnt offering, and arose and went to the place of which God had told him.

—Genesis 22:1–3

Then they came to the place of which God had told him. And Abraham built an altar there and placed the wood in order; and he bound Isaac his son and laid him on the altar, upon the wood. And Abraham stretched out his hand and took the knife to slay his son. But the Angel of the Lord called to him from heaven and said, "Abraham, Abraham!" So he said, "Here I am." And He said, "Do not lay your hand on the lad, or do anything to him; for now I know that you fear God, since you have not withheld your son, your only son, from Me."

—Genesis 22:9–12

Abraham trusted God so much that he was willing to obey Him. Although he did not know the reasons for the commands, he did know the heart of the One who was giving them. We find in the end that Isaac was not the sacrifice; instead, he was a prophetic shadow of the coming Messiah. So, how do you think Abraham was able to do this? Would any of us be able to obey to this extent? The truth is, Abraham knew his God. He had zero doubts about His nature and His character. He knew that God was setting him up for something beyond what he could comprehend. Abraham had promises and a covenant with God about his boy, and he knew that God was above all human limitations. Therefore, Abraham was able to put his trust in God and obey because of the relationship they had established together.

Have you ever heard this statement, "Just have blind faith"? Do you realize how unscriptural that is? There is no blind faith. Abraham knew God, had seen His nature, and had witnessed His character. With this foundation, he was willing and able to obey even when it took him to the limits of his understanding. He was able to relinquish control. As a believer, it is vital to spend time getting to know your Father, getting to know the Holy Spirit, and getting to know Jesus. The fruit of intimately knowing the Trinity makes obeying easy. It's so easy because you know exactly where His love is taking you. He's taking you into green pastures. He's taking you to still waters. He's taking you to a place where His rod and His staff are comforting you. He is walking you to the banqueting table. Take a moment and soak this truth in. God is wanting to take you to wonderful, wonderful places. Even if your carnal mind is struggling to understand, that does not mean it's not real. It is. If you know your Father, you can let go and trust Him fully and completely.

How was Abraham able to obey, and what can we learn from him? When we read about him, we see that he had a promise for a son, and his son was a miracle. Abraham also was promised nations, and he had seen God do miraculous things in his life. So he was confident that God was up to something that surpassed his ability to comprehend. Now, let's pause and apply this understanding to you. What is God up to in your life? What is God wanting to do in you? Where is God wanting to take you? He is actively leading you, and He wants you to know His ways.

Take a moment and check in on your heart. Are you able to let go of your earthly understanding and trust the leading of your loving God? If your honest answer is no, I challenge you as a friend to realize that there's something holding you back. Whether it be a hurt, a traumatic event, or the need to control that has locked up your heart, realize that it is keeping you from receiving the reality that God has good things for you. Maybe you need to resolve in your heart that God is a good God. Many people struggle with the truth that God is good. They can have a hard time comprehending and accepting this truth because they look at the things they have been through and think, *How could God be good if I went through this?* Sadly, for so many, the relationship they did or did not have with their earthly father built a false image of their heavenly Father. Remember that God has only good intentions, and the bad things that happened are the product of the fall and a broken world. He did not author evil and pain. God wants to bring order to where trauma has knocked you out of order and unity with Him. Jesus wants to bring you back into His loving order. I have found that when people's hearts are in unity with Him, there are no limits. So, if you are facing limits and restrictions, then have we just uncovered your answer?

What has God put in your heart that might not make sense to you? Can you recall the whispers of the Holy Spirit that you have heard—prophetic words and stirrings of your spirit and calling? How many times have you heard this: "I'm going to put that word on the shelf." The devil loves it when you take something from the heavenly realms and put it on a shelf. When are you ever going to take it off the shelf? When are you going to do something with it? We have so much stuff on the shelf. That's why we are not going anywhere. These words and stirrings are on a shelf waiting, and we are sitting on the shelf with them, collecting dust. Hopelessness and depression can come from abandoned dreams and forgotten prophetic words. Our relationship with Jesus restores hope and trust, and following His leadings becomes easy because we see the results in our life.

Let's start taking the ingredients down off that shelf and start baking some prophetic bread. God is waiting for us to do something with what He's already given us. However, when we get so trapped and caught up in hurt and control and trying to be in control of life, we find that we never step out to do anything. It's a spiritual and earthly deadlock! I say this because I believe trusting His leading is one of the biggest keys to unlocking us to move into our destiny. Remember, our ways of excusing ourselves from our destiny are not valid; we have not been disqualified. Our destiny has already been written by the pen of our Father, and it is ready to be implemented through us. Now, it's about releasing it and walking into it. It's about applying Psalm 23 to our lives. If you're not walking in the benefits of Psalm 23, then we need to uncover what is holding you back. This spiritual conclusion is different for everybody, yet the Holy Spirit is here right now to speak to you and reveal what you need to unlock your heart.

> *For the testimony of Jesus is the spirit of prophecy.*
> —**Revelation 19:10b**

Your life is a prophecy. Think about this for a moment with me. You don't need to get a new "word"; you *are* a "word," and you can deliver a word because Jesus is alive inside of you! When you declare and testify of Jesus, you are prophesying. Everything I'm sharing with you here; I'm prophesying to you. I'm literally prophesying to your spirit. As I declare Jesus, I am declaring your hope, your future, your resolution, and your destiny! When you are at your job, with your family, or at the store, you are a walking prophecy. You are living as a testimony of the saving power of Jesus. You might think that prophecy is just telling somebody's future, but what if the future was already written down? What if it was really easy for you to tell others about it? What God has done for you is proof of what He will do for them. God has healing! He wants to restore! He is faithful! He has been and will be forever and ever.

I am releasing this message to you because God is trying to propel you forward. He is stirring you and putting a fire inside you. What's keeping you from stepping out? You have to begin to fill in the blanks. As a believer, you must put in the work to uncover these areas of the soul. If you don't, you will miss out on all that God has for you. Remember, you cannot uncover spiritual truth with your soul. You need to activate your spirit to walk in the spirit. You do so by praying in the Spirit as much as possible in order to tip the scales within yourself. This is also why we need to talk about letting go—letting the soul go to see the Spirit with clarity.

> *Therefore we also, since we are surrounded by so great a cloud of witnesses, let us lay aside every weight, and the sin which so easily ensnares us, and let us run with endurance the race that is set before us, looking unto Jesus, the author and finisher of our faith, who for the joy that was set before Him endured the cross, despising the shame, and has sat down at the right hand of the throne of God.*
>
> **—Hebrews 12:1–2**

You were made for fire and heavenly passion. You were made to be alive and full of life. You were created in the image and the nature of God. Everyone was made to be a living testimony and a living prophecy to this generation. You were created for that purpose. The portion of Scripture we just read holds a lot of answers for us. We can let go of every sin and every wound that has pierced us. Think about this progression with me if you are struggling with an addiction or habitual problem. Many never overcome that kind of problem because it is a result or the fruit of a broken place within them. A high fever is the result of an infection within the body. A check engine light is proof of an engine problem. A broken life is the result of something broken in someone's heart and soul. The manifestations of addiction and sin are the result of brokenness and are the enemy's work to destroy the believer. If you don't resolve the cause, you will not change the results.

Recognizing the results or fruit of our lives and understanding the sources is the key to achieving permanent healing and deliverance. If you need a little more convincing, stop and be honest with yourself. Do you want to sin? Do you want an addiction? Of course not! You want freedom and life. Your true desires are for healing and wholeness. Your desires are not the problem; the problem is what happened to you to derail those desires. I know you want to choose hope and healing. Your will and heart want God and His plans, yet something broken is overriding your will and self-control and causing you to choose brokenness and sin while fighting a war inside.

Yelling at yourself and using willpower is never a path to permanent healing and deliverance. Rather you should go back to this point: *we must let go of every wound*. Wounds are the products of this fallen world through sin. They are gateways to addictions, as the addictions seem to help or provide temporary relief. That's why, if your strategy to overcome is beating yourself up and telling yourself, "I'm never going to do this again," you will live on repeat in this area. Striving to maintain control with willpower will never get you anywhere. Willpower, at best, will only give you a few weeks or days of holding out until the cycle repeats. It will last for a short time, and then you will fall again, right? The honest evaluation is that you are hooked because the enemy has you in this cycle of pain, self-comfort, shame, and a contest of willpower. What's even more evil is that the enemy is the one who set you up with this wound in the first place. He set you up with a wound so that you would fall into a bondage within the array of options that lucifer offers. His goal is for you to never get out of it. However, you can overcome and begin to reverse engineer this process in your life. If you are looking in your heart and life and see a broken place, a cycle, or an addiction, you're not going to overcome it by controlling it. You are going to overcome it by letting go and healing it.

Many great men and women of God have understood this secret; they knew how to unhook and disconnect themselves from the things that had become anchors to their lives. For many, these anchors took hold when they were children during neglect, pain, loss, and other horrible things that happened. A missing or absent parent is enough in itself to derail a person who, as an adult, is held back mentally and emotionally in places that he or she never developed and matured. Many are held hostage in these moments of time that are now driving the subconscious decisions they make every day. This is where the enemy starts people on a path of destruction. The key to knowing and resolving these times and places is to let the Holy Spirit navigate in our lives and bring us to new moments that happen to perform the most beautiful and loving surgery. Many, if not most, do not take this journey of healing and restoration. It is the fallen human nature to operate out of self-reliance, and when that tendency is paired with pain, people have a massive roadblock to obtaining their destiny. If an individual has encountered sexual abuse in any form, this principle is especially true. For most people, this hidden and painful place is dealt with by blaming themselves. Many in the body of Christ operate out of self-reliance because of the snares of the enemy's trauma. They live exhausted and frustrated as a result. They live just coping and surviving because they are still just trying to cope with and survive all they have gone though. What if the key to healing and living again was just setting themselves free from blame and shame because, at the beginning, it was not their fault?

If you want to know why people just get up and leave one church to go to another, it's usually because they are looking for something that people will never be able to give them. They don't like this pastor, or they don't like that person, or the music, or the church structure. This is why people get into all these worthless soul debates—in their broken lives, they are trying to control circumstances and other broken people whom they can never control. The answer to their pain is not in the church building or the people; it's in the delivering power of Jesus Christ and Him alone.

We gain order, God's order, back in our life by healing and letting go—by freeing ourselves from the things that we have become bound to. So, let's set your heart free with God's love and this revelation: it's not all your fault; this was done to you.

Have you considered how Jesus thinks and feels about you? Jesus is in the business of letting go. Remember, He knew every detail of your thoughts, words, and actions, and He was still able to let go of your past. Did you know that He was also able to let go of your failures and shortcomings? Do you realize that Jesus was able to let go of your Ishmaels? By "Ishmaels" I mean the times you tried to do something in your own way and made mistakes that cost you. Your Father God has let go of all those things because of the blood and sacrifice of Jesus. If anybody is holding on to something, it's not Him. And if it's not Him, then it's you! Bingo! Right here, right now, in this moment, is a revelation that you can embrace forever. The Holy Spirit is doing this work in us together. This truth of God's heart and nature changes us, and it delivers us from everything we have been through. Jesus was able to let go of everything. The Father was able to let go of everything. Now it's up to you to truly let go of whatever has ensnared your heart. Your next decision will determine your direction.

Your sins are "as far as the east is from the west" (Psalm 103:12a). You're never going to find them. They're gone. This frees you now to invest in your destiny and resolve the entrapping thoughts you fight with. The records and files you keep going through don't even exist in Heaven. The healing you have been praying for in your physical body, your emotions, and your mind will happen when you allow yourself to let go of your past. Your body is just responding to a broken heart; yet it is ready to heal and live again.

Are you praying for a miracle? Here is what I believe the Holy Spirit wants you to know: it is time to let go of Ishmael. Many people believe that because we have made mistakes, we must pay for them and carry them. Do you feel like your mistakes have somehow wrecked your future, leaving you without hope of change and new life? Think about the stories in the Scriptures. Do you know how many actions and decisions were done wrong, but God and His grace made it right? Let us remove the excuses we have for why we can't let go.

You have no argument for holding on to the pain of the past. Biblically, you have no foundation to hold on to anything in your past. Unhook yourself mentally and emotionally, letting go of every mistake and bad choice that you made, because your spirit has already let go. There is no doubt that you did fall short and that you did make a mess, just like every one of us has. But the reality is that you cannot resolve it on your own; you must accept His gift of freedom that you struggle with taking. It comes down to receiving this gift and accepting that He did for you what you could never do on your own. You may think to yourself, *I'm going to protect my future by making sure I never do that again*, only to end up doing it again because it comes back to that issue of control. It comes back to willpower. If you're trying to stop and prevent a cycle by being in control, you will live as a victim of the cycle.

God has so much for you, and your heart knows it. When I say that God has set a table of blessings for you, your spirit says, "Yes!" But in the moments of letting hope come alive, we sometimes start to fall off the cliff of emotions and thoughts of all the reasons you are disqualified, right? So, let's deal with the mental and emotional cliffs that the demonic forces love to try to hold us over, the landmines that are lying in the soil of our lives. Pause for a moment and think about these barriers and traps with me. What are the cliffs that you face? What are the mental and emotional landmines that you keep stepping on? Allow the Holy Spirit to identify them and take them out. You need His love, not the whip you keep hitting yourself with. Let His love become your deliverance.

If you have done hurtful and horrible things to people, friends, or family, can you forgive yourself today? Jesus wants you to forgive yourself because, in Heaven, your slate is completely clean. Here's what I know as a pastor. If you have done awful things, it's probably because somebody did horrible things to you. Those actions set something in motion that was never supposed to be. You were first the victim.

I am so sorry for all that you have been through. I know that, for many, life has been very hard. I know that it hurts so much to open these places up, yet doing so is vital for true deliverance and healing to take place. You have spent so much time running from the pain; now, break the cycle and run toward that pain with Jesus. Let Jesus hold you and love on you right now. Many never overcome what you have overcome, yet you are here today, letting God transform your life. In His healing, there is unlimited hope and destiny for you. You can allow Him to go into these deep places because He is safe and has only healing for you. Breathe and pray this with me: "Jesus, come into every place of pain. Take over every moment of trauma. Turn the ashes of my life into the beauty of the destiny You are now placing in me. In Jesus's name, Amen."

What will you gain through this process of transformation? You will gain the real you when you begin to let go—the light, happy, excited, and incredible you. With Jesus, you recover the pieces of you that were lost. You feel broken because of the parts of your personality and life that were lost along the way. But here is the most incredible truth: Jesus knows every piece of you that is lost, where it was lost, and how to make you whole again. You are not permanently broken; you just are temporarily in pieces. Jesus restores it all through the Holy Spirit. The following are steps I would recommend you use to obtain the permanent healing and restoration of the real you that Father God breathed at your creation.

1. When you see a broken place, immediately pray and ask for revelation about its source.

2. Pray in tongues and let the Spirit lead you into His love and a path for resolution.

3. Pray in line with the revelation you are receiving.

4. Forgive and allow healing to sweep through you. Choose to side with God's Word and His love for you. This is the moment of letting go and receiving wholeness.

5. Fill your heart with thanksgiving and worship. Let joy and love revive this place you have now taken back. Let God's love and His Word minister to you about this specific place in your life.

Apply and repeat these steps as much as needed. Yes, it can be this simple!

Use this process daily, as I do. You don't always need to call your pastor or a prophet when you see areas that need healing come up in your life. You have full access to the same God and power that they do. As you begin to apply and walk this process out, you will gain continued transformation. How do you know you have been healed? You'll know when you walk into the room—into a place in your heart—and although you remember the pain that was there before, now it is sparkly clean. You can sit and drink your coffee there and begin to testify of what God did in you! That room is not painful anymore; that room is now a testimony. Your control of this space is gone; order and peace now fill it, and you are complete. It is the most beautiful and wonderful moment when you see how far God has brought you, and you can declare, "I am healed! I thank You that You have made all things new in my life!" (See 2 Corinthians 5:17.)

PRAY TO OUR FATHER WITH ME:

Father, today, I give You full access to every room and every layer of my heart. I have lost pieces of my heart and my identity. I cannot fight to hold it all together anymore. I give You control and ask You for Your order in my life. I choose You, and I choose to heal. I receive forgiveness and the revelation of Your love. For every hurt and wound that I don't see, begin to open the doors of my heart and clean out the clutter. I believe there is hope and a future for me. I believe that I have a destiny. Because of the blood You shed for me, I take back all that was stolen from me. In Jesus's name, Amen.

Now take some time to answer the following questions.

**What are two key points you are taking from
this chapter and applying to your life?**

_____

_____

_____

_____

**In what areas of trauma and brokenness are you
giving up control so you receive God's order?**

_____

_____

_____

_____

**What is the Holy Spirit saying to you from this chapter
that you want to invest more prayer and study into?**

_____

_____

_____

_____

CHAPTER 7

YOUR SEAT AT THE TABLE

*Like an apple tree among the trees of the woods,
so is my beloved among the sons. I sat down in his
shade with great delight, and his fruit was sweet to
my taste. He brought me to the banqueting house,
and his banner over me was love.*

—Song of Solomon 2:3–4

In Heaven there is a table, and at that table there is a seat just for you. It is reserved for you alone, and no one else can or will take it. No one can sit in that seat but you. You are made in your Father's image, and He has made a place for you because He loves you and values you. You might "know" this truth, but when you go through this journey to receive healing for all that you have been through, you must become fully convinced that He loves you, that it's not too late, and that He will walk you into everything He has put in your heart. Please know that it can take time to be healed and convinced of this truth because this world is broken, and you are fighting its evil currents. The currents of the fall are working hard every day to convince you that you "belong" with them and that what the Bible says is only for some. These evil currents want you to believe that "some" does not include you. Let's also add that these currents want you to believe that you are no different from all the other broken things and that you should just accept your place in this world. This is why it is so important to read Scriptures about your value and identity. God's Word will establish you so you can identify with your true home and Father. Focusing on who you are in Christ and understanding the believer's inheritance is how you are delivered from this world's grip. Just read this Scripture about your salvation and inheritance:

> *Blessed be the God and Father of our Lord Jesus Christ, who according to His abundant mercy has begotten us again to a living hope through the resurrection of Jesus Christ from the dead, to an inheritance incorruptible and undefiled and that does not fade away, reserved in heaven for you, who are kept by the power of God through faith for salvation ready to be revealed in the last time.*
>
> **—1 Peter 1:3–5**

Salvation is the beginning, the starting point, as a believer. If you live your whole life at the starting line, you will live unfulfilled and disappointed. You were made to create and build, which is discovered and fueled by your heavenly inheritance! You were made to bear fruit and endless joy, not to survive or just make it. The value system of this world cannot place a correct value on you because this world is not your home. The truth is, the world does not understand the value your Father has placed in you, just like it could not understand Jesus when He was here. Your healing and fulfillment are found in the treasures of your Father's inheritance that He has provided for you. It is found at His table of acceptance and in His endless pleasure over you. He wants you to be with Him!

Do you ever have thoughts like, I want to do something for God, or I wish I could help certain groups of people? I am confident you do because that is the Holy Spirit stirring inside you. Those thoughts are the beginning of big things in the kingdom through you. The vital moments of God birthing a work in you and presenting your calling can be lost by you failing to renew your mind. If you have an incorrect understanding of how God sees you and feels about you, then you will not take the next steps toward what God is stirring in you. A broken identity will abort the callings of the Holy Spirit because it will cause you to side with the reasons you should not or cannot follow Him.

I remember, when I was in Bible college, I had some wrong mindsets about how Jesus wanted to use my life. I so wanted the power of God to flow through me and for explosive miracles to happen. I would only look for the "big" and the "notable" acts of God. As I grew and matured, I was blown away by the fact that I was seeing miracles every day. They were right in front of me, and my Father was causing fruit to flourish through me. I began to see that the more healing and renewing with the Word of God I received, the more I could see Him and His hand in my life. Sometimes we think He is not doing great works, but the fact is our minds are clouded and are not seeing clearly. Right now, He is doing miracles in your life. Many of those miracles are little adjustments and leadings that keep you on track, safe, and under His covering.

God's love for us is the filter that cleans out all the garbage of this world. We must take the dirty water and air of this world that has gotten inside us and begin to let the Holy Spirit and the Word of God cleanse the atmosphere of our hearts and minds.

I love imagining the table of the Lord. Take a moment and picture His table with me. Imagine a massive and exceptional table that is full of food! All of us are dining together, eating and drinking with our Father, the King of all kings! No one is left out or rejected. We are all wanted and loved by Him. Our differences have been melted away by the radiance of His heart for us. The sacrifice of Jesus bought us back to Him!

Thank You, Jesus, for the blood!
Thank You, Father, for Your love!
Thank You, Holy Spirit, for revealing all to us!

Now here is a heart test. Did you think, when you imagined this table, I cannot wait to be there with Him one day! Or did you think, I am seated with Him right now enjoying His glory! Friend, we don't have to wait; we have full access today!

But God, who is rich in mercy, because of His great love with which He loved us, even when we were dead in trespasses, made us alive together with

Christ (by grace you have been saved), and raised us up together, and made us sit together in the heavenly places in Christ Jesus.

—Ephesians 2:4–6

I share this truth with you because our minds need to be renewed so we don't miss out on all God has for us. In this life, our soul has to be thoroughly cleaned out and continuously transformed to be able to receive what Heaven has for us. It is the vital component many miss in learning how to receive good gifts from our loving Father God. In what ways do you need to renew your mind so you can receive from Abba Father?

If you are not seeing good fruit in your life, then something you're believing is stopping healthy growth. If you're not walking in what God has for you, I guarantee that a hurt, a wound, a trauma, or a mindset is keeping you from walking on the path that Jesus has available for you personally. If you don't walk on that path, then not only will you miss out, but also other people will go without what you are called to give them. If you don't take your seat, then that seat will be empty. It's the same thing on this earth as it is in Heaven. You are loved, called, and chosen, and you are so needed for this harvest.

Yes, you may have messed up, but you can change all that through Jesus. You have the power to decide and accept the fact that you are made in the image of God. Your chair is reserved and waiting for you to come and sit with Him. Being made in the image of God means that you can create. Your future can be created and implemented today with Jesus. The Holy Spirit is now speaking and giving you direction in your spirit as you read. Your part is to take hold of this truth and begin to build. Remember, every new building begins with the first shovelful of dirt. Fulfillment of your heart's desires and your destiny begins the same way. Pause and take this first step into your new season in your heart right now.

Now is your time to remove the obstacles, the objects that have stolen your worship and your heart. They are traps to steal your destiny, which was fully paid for by the blood of Jesus. All of us have a calling, and your crafty enemy is fighting to try to rob both God and you. He wants to steal what was written in Heaven about you and the people you are assigned to. If you don't go out and do what you're called to do, others will lack what you have to give them. You and I are not the only ones who are the victims when we don't do what we're called to do. You have been restored to the Father, and He only asks that you now replicate this gift and help others to find this same hope.

> *Now all things are of God, who has reconciled us to Himself through Jesus Christ, and has given us the ministry of reconciliation, that is, that God was in Christ reconciling the world to Himself, not imputing their trespasses to them, and has committed to us the word of reconciliation.*
> —2 Corinthians 5:18–19

Every single one of us is called to this ministry of reconciliation. State this out loud:

"I am called to the ministry of reconciliation."

Maybe you were told that because you are a woman, you don't have a ministry or calling. Man or woman, perhaps it's your past that you feel has disqualified you. The Bible, however, simply says that you are called to a ministry of reconciliation. You receive reconciliation and then help minister this good news to others. Last time I checked, our feelings do not add addendums to the Scripture or disqualify us from this calling. You are called to restore people to Jesus Christ. So, let me now welcome you to the ministry! Heaven has been waiting for you, and this generation needs you desperately! Change your thinking so you can change your fruit. This is what James, Paul, Peter, John, and all the disciples and apostles learned from Jesus.

> But you are a chosen generation, a royal priesthood, a holy nation, His own special people, that you may proclaim the praises of Him who called you out of darkness into His marvelous light.
>
> —1 Peter 2:9

If you're out of darkness and in the marvelous light, then that means you are truly out of the darkness and no longer wandering around with blindness. You can now start to identify and value yourself with this marvelous light that you have received. Can you let your faith grab hold and begin to identify yourself as a treasure? You are His precious workmanship.

I find that this topic is the crux that either keeps people out of their calling or launches them into it. Whether you have been in ministry for fifty years or just gave your life to Jesus, I pray that your heart receives this revelation. You must begin to believe that what the Bible says about you really is for you. We are all very comfortable telling other people we are fine when we really are not. But if somebody is going through a hard time, we should be able to help that person and share with him or her, "God's got you. He's got a destiny for you." We also should be able to find ways to help that person. Having practical ways to show God's love is so vital. It is amazing how a warm meal and a hug can change everything.

We need the Holy Spirit to come and remove the "furniture" of this world that has occupied the soul. It's time for Jesus to set up His kingdom inside you in a whole new way. You can take the first steps by studying and digesting the Scripture, by letting the Word get in you so deep that it corrects your very DNA. The Word is your secret weapon, and it cuts up all the demonic vines that have grown around you. God's Word can remove the limitations that feel like gravity's trying to push brokenness down on you. It may feel like everything wants to steal, kill, and destroy you, but when you have the Word of God flowing like a river inside you, your words have become His words. You reject demonic attacks and rejection with God's authority through your mouth. You begin to say things like, "I am His treasure! I am a chosen priesthood. I am called." Make your decision, then plan that you will begin to know the Word in a whole new way. Plan that you will take your seat of acceptance and adoption today. You are no longer waiting; you are obtaining in Jesus's name!

PRAY WITH ME:

Holy Spirit, I ask You for revelation. Clean out my mind and my emotions. Reveal to me every way I am not seeing our relationship correctly. Change my thinking so I can see all that You have for me today. Let me have new eyes to see what You have put before me. Help me to reject the negative and deflating thoughts of the enemy. Flood me with revelation light, so that I am never the same. In Jesus's holy name, Amen.

Take a moment to have your personal "identity check" with the following questions.

Do I see myself seated in heavenly places, or do I feel like I am not good enough yet?

_____

_____

_____

_____

What is keeping me from believing that I have a calling and ministry?

_____

_____

_____

_____

In what simple ways would I like to share the love of God with others?

_____

_____

_____

_____

CHAPTER 8

LOST AND NOW FOUND

Have you ever experienced a riptide or a rip current in the ocean? It is an unexpected yet powerful force. One moment you are having fun and enjoying the waves and the sun. Then the next you feel your feet being pulled out from under you. A riptide can get so strong that it can take you out into the ocean, and no matter how well you swim, you cannot overpower the ocean. You can go from having a great time to thinking you're going to die rather quickly. It's scary... very scary. I know, for I've been there and been swept out by its force. That is what the world wants to do to you. It wants to sweep you off your feet and keep you in the false identity of a cheap garage sale item. It wants to keep that low price sticker on you. Then it wants to send someone by to say, "You're not even worth that. I'll give fifty cents for you." This devaluation may be what's happening at your job. This may be what's happening with people around you. Maybe it has all been designed to erode the coastline of your heart and life.

The rip current of this broken world wants to pull you farther and farther away from your Father and your destiny. It is the reason most believers feel unfulfilled. You have a calling on your life, and it is fueled with purpose—but the current is pulling you away from what your spirit knows God has for you.

Now, lest you think that this calling means you are to be behind a piano or a pulpit, let me assure you that's not always what it means. I'll be honest with you, sharing that prophetic word with that waitress I mentioned in the first chapter made my whole week. I could give prophetic words all day long, and I would be just fine and satisfied. If I can see the tangible power of God transforming a life... that's everything to me! Everyone should be prophesying. Everyone can help people. It is time for all of us to declare the Word of God over our families, coworkers, and communities.

Again, the kingdom of heaven is like a merchant seeking beautiful pearls, who, when he had found one pearl of great price, went and sold all that he had and bought it.

—Matthew 13:45–46

Jesus is this pearl of great price, and you are His pearl of great price. When you read these verses, you can easily think, Oh, that's nice, but it's for someone else. However, I want you to understand the depth of this passage and its meaning for you. It is time to stop disqualifying yourself.

Let's go deeper in studying the pearls of these verses. In our current generation, we have a lot of fake pearls, and their value is very different. Pearls in Jesus's time, however, were more valuable than diamonds. When Jesus was sharing this parable, He was communicating to the people in a way they could best understand.

All pearls in the New Testament times were real and extremely valuable. There was no way to manufacture or produce them then like we can now. You either had the real thing, or you didn't.

To harvest a pearl in those times, divers would tie one end of a rope around themselves and attach the other end of the rope to a rock. They would throw both themselves and the rock overboard and scrummage in the mud where there were eels and sharks and other sea creatures. They didn't have snorkel gear or any equipment to help them stay underwater. Instead, they had to hold their breath while the rock acted as their anchor on the bottom of the ocean floor.

These factors caused pearl diving to be one of the most dangerous things one could do. I don't know about you, but on my "bucket list," I don't have, "tie a rope around myself with a rock on the other end and go forty feet down into the sea."

The divers would hunt these oysters, and it was common to find only one pearl in as many as 10,000 oysters. This meant they would spend days getting up, tying the rock on, jumping in, plunging into the mud, and hunting for oysters. They would find some and go back up, open them up, and be met with disappointment. They would do this for days, trying to find pearls. Pearls were so expensive that only the pharaohs and the super wealthy would have them. They used the pearls to show their wealth, power, and status. The ladies would put them in their hair as a symbol of their position and royalty. Basically, only the elite had them; the rest of the world did not.

Pearls were everything. Pearls distinguished value. They distinguished wealth. They distinguished royalty. So, when Jesus included pearls in His parables, it meant that what He was communicating had a great amount of depth and meaning to the people personally. Jesus declared that He is the pearl of great price to us. If we could somehow fully comprehend the value of Jesus, the value of His blood, and the value of the cross in this life...what total freedom and fullness of His power we would have!

> *Do not give what is holy to the dogs; nor cast your pearls before swine, lest they trample them under their feet, and turn and tear you in pieces.*
> —**Matthew 7:6**

This verse tells you why you should not throw your pearls before swine. Pearls, like you, were not made for the mud. Pearls were not made for pigs. Pearls were made for royalty. That's why there are times in your life when you feel like you don't fit in. That's why you sometimes feel like things are not right or are just wrong around you. It's because, in the Garden of Eden, people were made to be in His perfect presence forever. You were created in His image. You were made to worship the Father forever. You were made to be clean and pure and spotless. You were made for holiness and glory. You were not made for mud, dirt, and sin.

When Jesus died on the cross, He restored our lives and value. He restored our identity back to the original intent. He restored our worth. Let's consider, then, that if all has been restored to our spirit, where did things start to go wrong? The answer is, our spirit is flawless, but our soul lives in this broken world with brokenness all around us. Friend, this is a love of God moment. You don't need to beat yourself into submission to be a follower of Jesus. You just need to see the value He restored to you and begin to live out of that revelation.

I have four daughters. If any one of my girls are doing something that I don't agree with, I don't smack her upside the head and say, "You should know better and stop it!" Rather, I say to my daughter, "Baby girl, you are better than this. You have so much more potential than this. Because of your value and your worth, let's bring you up higher." Many of us get that condemning "top down" feeling about God because people treated us with harshness and judgment. We get out our Bible and say, "Bring out the whip, Jesus! Go get them!" Or, "Just hit me, and let's get this over with." We must reject the thinking that God deals with us in the same way people have dealt with us.

Let's renew our minds and receive the truth that we are pearls, as are the people in our lives. He wants to love each of us that same way. Let Him love you today!

Jesus's intentions are for you to understand what He's done for you and to bring you up into the heavenly places. He wants you seated next to Him in the thrones of Heaven, not living in the mud and the yuck of this world. He desires the same for your brothers and sisters. Let's help everyone we can! We are all sons and daughters!

When someone says something mean or negative to hurt you, that is not God. God loves you, and He has a special plan for you. You were made in God's image. You have free will, and you can choose to do right, or you can choose to do wrong. If people do something that hurts you, they are choosing the wrong thing, and they are not representing God. Believers, as Christians, are the ones who will help to show the world who God really is. You are His ambassador, and how you treat people will determine how they see the Father.

Jesus is the pearl of great price in Matthew 13. Imagine the most beautiful, stunning, exquisite pearl in the universe. That is our Jesus. He is everything, and He is here to help you. He's going to help you with your whole life. He is going to teach you and lead you. Why? Receive this truth: Jesus sees you as His pearl.

Jesus sees you as precious. He sees you as perfect by the blood. He sees you as priceless—because you are.

Now is the day and time to let this truth transform your thinking, actions, and decisions. It's time for you to see how God sees you. Reject the evil and horrible things people have said and done to you. Those things have been like an anchor, a label, a brick wall that stops you from living full of the Spirit. They have kept you from receiving and being free. Think about this: Heaven is always sending and delivering, but you have not been able to receive because all these things have clogged your ears, your mind, and your heart. They have hindered you from hearing what God is saying to you. Your healing begins when you realize that you are a treasure, when you understand your worth. That is when you are safe to heal.

Your journey begins today. It begins now. Your value and identity have been revealed as we have taken this journey together through this book. Your part is now to partner with the Holy Spirit and invest truth in yourself. Worship the Father! Pray and pour out your heart every day! Purposefully do things to build yourself up and strengthen yourself in the Holy Spirit (see Jude 20). As you uncover the areas that need more truth and wholeness, take the time to let the love of God work in you. You can do it! Even if it takes a year or twenty-five years, you're worth it. He sees you as worth it. Isn't it time that you now believe how He sees you and feels about you? I believe that, today, your new course has been set and that you are never turning back.

PRAY WITH ME:

Father, I thank You that I am set apart. I am chosen by You. I see the valuable treasure that I have in You, and I see that I am Your treasure. Thank You for finding me and placing me in Your kingdom. Reveal in me the destiny and plan that You have for my life. Let me begin to walk in it today in small and big ways for You, never going back. In Jesus's name, Amen!

Let's pause and reflect on what we have uncovered in this chapter.

**In what ways will you live and think differently
now that you know you are His treasure?**

_____

_____

_____

_____

**In what ways have you felt that God wants to use you? What
people and places make your heart burn with God's love?**

_____

_____

_____

_____

**What words and understanding do you have to
describe your value and relationship with God?**

_____

_____

_____

_____

CHAPTER 9

IMPARTATION PRAYER

As we have been on a journey through this book, I know you have been receiving revelation for your life. Pray this prayer with me and believe our loving Father will do an incredible work in you. Declare it with me:

Father, I ask You now that You would begin to do a transformational work inside of me, that You would begin to do a powerful healing inside of me. Lord, I ask that You break up any hard ground and tear down any walls or barriers that have been built up by brokenness or trauma. God, I ask that You would cause my heart to be transformed from stone into soft, tender flesh. Mold me and shape me, Jesus. This world is so broken, and I ask You to take all the brokenness out of me so that I can be effective. I thank You that today, I am taking a big step. I am not believing the lies anymore. I am not an impostor. I am the righteousness of Christ. I am Your treasure, and You have wonderful plans for me. I begin to walk in them today.

I declare that from this moment forward, I am going to step into the next phase of my life. I am going to walk out of the past and walk into my future. Everything this broken world said I couldn't do; I am now going to say that I can do with Jesus. I reject that it is too late or that I am disqualified. I now declare, "Now is the time!"

Lord, evaporate my excuses with Your love.

Father, You are a miracle-working, powerful, wonderful God. And I thank You that You are taking those false price tags off me. I thank You that those price tags are coming off and that You are putting a new tag on me that says "Priceless! Priceless treasure!" And I declare that You are my priceless treasure!

Father, I thank You for everything You have done. I seal up this renewing work in every area of my being. I thank You, Lord, that I am going to receive a harvest.

Jesus, anything that's coming up in me right now because of reading this book and Your Word, I will not allow to cause me to shrink back. I will not shove it down and avoid it; but, Lord, give me the courage to face it, to bring it to You, to resolve it with Your truth and unending love. Lord, there's nothing too big that You can't heal. Lord, I thank You that I will begin to see my heavenly value, the value You have placed in me.

I speak acceleration. I declare that God will unfold all the potential and wonderful things inside me and cause me to make up for any missed time. I am now on track by the Spirit!

From now on, all I am going to see in the Spirit is green lights—no more yellows and no more red lights. My healing and destiny is now in full effect. For I am now "confident of this very thing, that He who has begun a good work in you will complete it until the day of Jesus Christ" (Philippians 1:6).

In the holy name of Jesus, Amen!

CHAPTER 10

TRANSFORMATION SCRIPTURES AND DECLARATIONS

These biblical declarations are for you to read and declare over your life as you renew your mind. Use these as the Holy Spirit brings continued healing and restoration to your life. You were made in the image of God, and you are called to do great things for the kingdom. His Word declares it!

I only do those things that please my Father today! (**John 8:29**)

I am complete in Him who is the head of all principality and power. (**Colossians 2:10**)

*I am surrounded by a shield
of favor.* (**Psalm 5:12**)

*I have forsaken all, taken up my cross,
and am following You.* (**Luke 14:26–33**)

I am alive with Christ. (**Ephesians 2:5**)

*My identity is rooted in being loved and
being a lover of God!* (**John 14:21**)

*I am free from the law of sin
and death.* (**Romans 8:2**)

*I thank You that as I seek You
with all my heart, I will find
You!* (**Jeremiah 29:11–13**)

*I ask, and it shall be given unto me; I
seek, and I shall find; I knock, and it
shall be opened to me.* (**Matthew 7:7 –8**)

I am far from oppression, and fear does not come near me. (Isaiah 54:14)

I abhor what is evil today, and I cling to that which is good. (Romans 12:9)

I walk in the wisdom of God today. (James 1:5)

You, Lord, are a shield for me; You are my glory and the One who lifts up my head. (Psalm 3:3)

I declare today that I love God with all my heart, mind, soul, and strength. (Luke 10:27)

I walk in the Spirit today, and I do not fulfill the lusts and desires of the flesh. (Galatians 5:16)

You have come that I would have life more abundantly. (John 10:10)

*I am born of God, and the evil one
does not touch me.* (1 John 5:18)

*I will not worry today or be
anxious.* (Philippians 4:6)

*I declare that the love of God has been
poured out in my heart by the Holy Spirit
who has been given to me.* (Romans 5:5)

*I am holy and without blame before Him
in love.* (1 Peter 1:16; Ephesians 1:4)

*I trust in the Lord today with all
my heart, and I do not lean on my
own understanding. In all my ways,
I acknowledge Him, and He directs
my paths.* (Proverbs 3:5–6)

I will pray without ceasing.
(1 Thessalonians 5:17)

I have the mind of Christ.
(Philippians 2:5; 1 Corinthians 2:16)

*I receive the fullness of God's love
today!* **(Ephesians 3:17–19)**

*You work all things together
for good because I love You and
am called according to Your
purposes.* **(Romans 8:28)**

*I have the peace of God that passes all
understanding.* **(Philippians 4:7)**

*You are keeping me in perfect
peace because my mind is stayed
on You.* **(Isaiah 26:3)**

*I have the Greater One living in me;
greater is He who is in me than he
who is in the world.* **(1 John 4:4)**

I declare today that nothing is too hard or impossible for God. (Luke 1:37)

I walk in the strength of the joy of the Lord today. (Nehemiah 8:10)

I declare today that His banner over me is love, love, love! (Song of Solomon 2:4)

I call unto the Lord, and He answers me and shows me great and mighty things! (Jeremiah 33:3)

I walk in the prophetic today. (1 Corinthians 14:1)

I hear the voice of God today. (John 10:4–5)

I walk in divine appointments. (Psalm 37:23)

I have received the gift of righteousness and reign as a king in life through Jesus Christ. (**Romans 5:17**)

The blessings of God have overtaken me! (**Deuteronomy 28:2**)

As I wait on the Lord today, my strength is renewed, and I mount up with wings like eagles. I run and do not grow weary, and I walk and do not faint. (**Isaiah 40:31**)

This is the day that the Lord has made, and I will rejoice and be glad in it! (**Psalm 118:24**)

I have received the spirit of wisdom and revelation in the knowledge of Jesus, the eyes of my understanding being enlightened. (**Ephesians 1:17–18**)

I am confident that He who has begun a good work in me will complete it until the day of Jesus Christ. (**Philippians 1:6**)

I have the tongue of the learned, and I know how to speak a word in season. (**Isaiah 50:4**)

I walk in the Isaiah 61 mandate today. (**Isaiah 61**)

I have received the power of the Holy Spirit to lay hands on the sick and see them recover, to cast out demons, and to speak with new tongues. I have power over all the power of the enemy, and nothing shall by any means harm me. (**Mark 16:17–18; Luke 10:17,19**)

I am free from all condemnation because I am in Christ Jesus. (**Romans 8:1**)

*I thank You that everything that
I set my hand to do is blessed!*
(Deuteronomy 28:12)

*I have put off the old man and have
put on the new man, which is renewed
in knowledge after the image of Him
who created me.* (Colossians 3:9–10)

*I put on the whole armor of God
today.* (Ephesians 6:11–17)

*I declare that no weapon formed
against me or my family today will
prosper, and every tongue that rises
up against us in judgment shall
be condemned.* (Isaiah 54:17)

*I present my body today as a living
sacrifice, holy, acceptable to God, which
is my reasonable service.* (Romans 12:1)

I will not be conformed to this world,
but I will be transformed by the
renewing of my mind. (**Romans 12:2**)

I have given, and it is given to me;
good measure, pressed down, shaken
together, and running over, people
give into my bosom. (**Luke 6:38**)

I can quench all the fiery darts
of the wicked one with my shield
of faith. (**Ephesians 6:16**)

I can do all things through
Christ Jesus who gives me
strength. (**Philippians 4:13**)

I shall do even greater works than
Christ Jesus. (**John 14:12**)

I will bless the Lord at all times;
His praise shall continually be in
my mouth. (**Psalm 34:1**)

I am God's child, for I am born again of the incorruptible seed of the Word of God, which lives and abides forever. (1 Peter 1:23)

I am a person after God's own heart! (Acts 13:22)

I am God's workmanship, created in Christ for good works. (Ephesians 2:10)

I am a new creature in Christ. (2 Corinthians 5:17)

I am a spirit being—alive to God. (1 Thessalonians 5:23; Romans 6:11)

I am a believer, and the light of the Gospel shines in my mind. (2 Corinthians 4:4)

I declare that my family is free of debt! (Philippians 4:19)

I am a doer of the Word, and I am blessed in my actions. (James 1:22,25)

I am a joint heir with Christ. (Romans 8:17)

I am more than a conqueror through Him who loves me. (Romans 8:37)

I am an overcomer by the blood of the Lamb and the word of my testimony. (Revelation 12:11)

I am a partaker of His divine nature. (2 Peter 1:3–4)

I am an ambassador for Christ. (2 Corinthians 5:20)

I am the righteousness of God in Jesus Christ. (2 Corinthians 5:21)

*I am part of a chosen generation,
a royal priesthood, a holy nation, and
a purchased people.* (**1 Peter 2:9**)

*I am the temple of the Holy Spirit; I am
not my own.* (**1 Corinthians 6:19**)

*I am the head and not the tail; I
am above only and not beneath.*
(**Deuteronomy 28:13**)

I am the salt of the earth.
(**Matthew 5:13**)

I am the light of the world.
(**Matthew 5:14**)

*I am His elect, full of mercy, kindness,
humility, and longsuffering.*
(**Romans 8:33; Colossians 3:12**)

*I owe only a debt of love to everyone
today.* (**Romans 13:8**)

*I am forgiven of all my sins
and washed in the blood.*
(Ephesians 1:7; 1 John 1:9)

*God has removed my sins as far as the
east is from the west.* (Psalm 103:12)

*I am delivered from the power of
darkness and translated into God's
Kingdom.* (Colossians 1:13)

*I am redeemed from the curse of sin,
sickness, and poverty.* (Galatians
3:13; Deuteronomy 28:15–68)

*I am firmly rooted, built up, established
in my faith, and overflowing with
gratitude.* (Colossians 2:7)

*I am called of God to be the voice of His
praise.* (2 Timothy 1:9; Psalm 66:8)

I am healed by the stripes of Jesus, and I walk in divine health.
(1 Peter 2:24; Isaiah 53:5)

I am raised up with Christ and am seated in heavenly places.
(Colossians 2:12; Ephesians 2:6)

I am greatly loved by God.
(Colossians 3:12; Romans 1:7; 1 Thessalonians 1:4; Ephesians 2:4)

I am strengthened with all might according to His glorious power. **(Colossians 1:11)**

I am submitted to God, and the devil flees from me because I resist him in the name of Jesus. **(James 4:7)**

I am strong in the Lord and in the power of His might. **(Ephesians 6:10)**

I press on toward the goal to win the prize to which God in Christ Jesus is calling me upward. (**Philippians 3:14**)

God has not given me a spirit of fear; He has given me power, love, and a sound mind. (**2 Timothy 1:7**)

It is not I who live, but Christ lives in me. (**Galatians 2:20**)

I declare that nothing shall separate me from the love of God! (**Romans 8:38–39**)

I keep myself in the love of God today! (**Jude 21**)

ABOUT THE AUTHOR

Mike Cowen is called to equip the body of Christ. He serves in many capacities to help bring healing and wholeness to believers so they can each fulfill their individual calling and destiny. Dr. Mike pastors at Antioch Community Fellowship, is a police chaplain, and the dean of students at Warrior Notes School of Ministry. He has been married to his wife, Christine, for more than 25 years. Together they have four daughters: Rebecca, Abigail, Meah, and Katelyn, and one incredible son-in-law, Owen.

You can contact Pastor Mike at:
mike@kevinzadai.org
Warriornotesschool.com
Antiochcommunitychurch.org

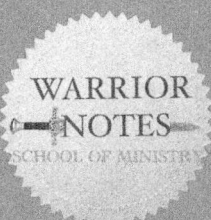

Printed in Great Britain
by Amazon

57054512R00066